Collins

Happy Handwriting

Practice Book 3

Series Editor: Dr Jane Medwell
Author: Stephanie Austwick

William Collins' dream of knowledge for all began with the publication of his first book in 1819. A self-educated mill worker, he not only enriched millions of lives, but also founded a flourishing publishing house. Today, staying true to this spirit, Collins books are packed with inspiration, innovation and practical expertise.

They place you at the centre of a world of possibility and give you exactly what you need to explore it.

Collins. Freedom to teach.

Published by Collins
An imprint of HarperCollins *Publishers*
The News Building, 1 London Bridge Street, London, SE1 9GF, UK

HarperCollins*Publishers*
Macken House, 39/40 Mayor Street Upper, Dublin 1, D01 C9W8, Ireland

Browse the complete Collins catalogue at collins.co.uk

10 9 8 7 6 5 4

ISBN 978-0-00-848582-5

British Library Cataloguing-in-Publication Data
A catalogue record for this publication is available from the British Library.

Series editor: Dr Jane Medwell
Author: Stephanie Austwick
Expert reviewer: Dr Mellissa Prunty
Publisher: Lizzie Catford
Product manager: Sarah Thomas
Project manager: Jayne Jarvis
Development editor: Jane Cotter
Copyeditor: Oriel Square Ltd
Proofreader: Oriel Square Ltd
Cover designer: Sarah-Leigh Wills at Happydesigner
Design template and icons: Sarah-Leigh Wills at Happydesigner
Cover artwork: Jouve India Pvt. Ltd.
Illustrations: Jouve India Pvt. Ltd.
Typesetter: Jouve India Pvt. Ltd.
Production controller: Alhady Ali
Printed in India by Multivista Global Pvt. Ltd.

This book contains FSC™ certified paper and other controlled sources to ensure responsible forest management.

For more information visit: www.harpercollins.co.uk/green

Write over and continue the pattern.

ilulull

Write over and copy the letters.

il it ti li tl ill ilt

Write over and copy the words.

till tile

title little

Remember to add the dots and cross strokes after joining each group of letters.

Write over and copy the words.

tall cat

pale take

Copy the old rhyme.

Pat-a-cake, pat-a-cake, baker's man,

Bake me a cake as fast as you can.

Are all the ascenders the correct height?

Write over and continue the pattern.

jlgty jlgty

Write over and copy the letters.

hly htly ing

Write over and copy the words.

my day by

say jump go

Write over and copy the words.

juggle garage

jolly yelling

Copy and complete each sentence with a suitable *ly* adverb.

The dog ran around ________.

The tree swayed ________.

The boy got out of bed ________.

Is l the correct height and is y the correct length?

Write over and continue the pattern.

ununun

Write over and copy the letters.

in um un

Write over and copy the words.

unwell insect

Write over and copy the words.

dim imagine

Unscramble the words and write them in the gaps. Then copy the completed sentences.

nfi	githn	uuunsla

The shark had a ________ on its back.

The owl only hunts at ________.

An elephant in a shop is ________.

Are **i**, **n** and **m** all the same height?

Write over and continue the pattern.

ininin

Write over and copy the letters.

ion ian ie

Remember to add the dot after joining all the letters.

Write over and copy the words.

lion vision

dictionary

Write over and copy the words.

division luckier

trail private

Join the letters from the first column with letters from the second column to make a word.

sta	in
tr	tion
tra	aining

Copy and complete the sentence using some of the words above.

The ______ is waiting at the ________.

Did you remember to put the dot on the i after you had finished the joins?

Write over and continue the pattern.

ee

Write over and copy the letters.

ei ey ea

Write over and copy the words.

their trolley

chimney dream

Write over and copy the words.

let rented

dinner cheese

Copy the poem. Take extra care with joining from the letter **e**.

A little kitten climbed a tree,

From the top, it could see the sea.

Are all your joins from **e** the same?

Write over and continue the pattern.

nlnlnl

Write over and copy the letters.

il it ak

Write over and copy the words.

pillow kitten

bite awake

Remember to add the dot after joining all the letters.

Write over and copy the words.

take bulb

shall glitter

Can you keep your pencil on the page when joining short and tall letters?

Copy the definitions and write the words they are describing.

1 Not short. t

2 Rubbish on the ground. l

3 The opposite of push. p

4 A maker of bread. b

Did you keep your pen or pencil on the paper when joining short and tall letters?

Write over and continue the pattern.

ly ly ly

Write over and copy the letters.

ly lly ny

Write over and copy the words.

sadly quickly

rainy funny

Write over and copy the words.

sly chilly tiny

Copy and complete these sentences, inserting the appropriate words.

rainy	sunny	finally

When it's ________ I go to the park.

When it's ________ I stay inside.

It's nice when the sun ________ shines.

Did you notice the join to **y** is the same from **l** and **n**?

Write over and continue the pattern.

ir ir ir

Write over and copy the letters.

er ur ir ar

Write over and copy the words.

bigger fur air

hair star car

Write over and copy the words.

Copy and complete the sentences, inserting the appropriate words.

finger	dinner	popular

1. I cut my __________ on some paper.

2. I sit down to eat my __________.

3. Football is __________ in my school.

It can be difficult to tell these r endings apart. Try arranging them in lists.

Write over and continue the pattern.

I.n.I.n.

Write over and copy the sentences.

"It is a letter," said the postperson.

"Thank you," replied Mrs White.

Copy the sentence.

"I can run fast," said the cheetah.

Copy and complete the sentences, adding inverted commas, commas and full stops.

I can fly high replied the eagle

We are all good at something said the lion

Do your inverted commas show exactly what is said?

Copy the sentence.

The friendly dog lifted its paw for the lady to shake.

How well do you think you have done in your writing?

My diagonal joins   

The height of my ascenders   

The length of my descenders   

Copy the poem.

Soon it will be Saturday

I'll stay at home and play all day.

How well do you think you have done in your writing?

My spaces between words   

My spaces between letters   

Write over and continue the pattern.

owow

Write over and copy the letters.

or ou ow

Write over and copy the words.

more hour

could throw

Write over and copy the words.

four fort door

Using letters *or ou ow oo*, complete the words then copy the whole sentence below.

The c jumped over the m n.

I get home at f r o'clock.

You get m e ice-cream in a c net.

Is your join from o the correct length?

Write over and continue the pattern.

olol

Write over and copy the letters.

ol ot ob

Write over and copy the words.

told rolled

rotten robber

Write over the words.

who what when where why

Copy the poem.

The tawny owl wakes when day
turns to night,

But where does it go when it starts
to get light?

Can you join wh? It's very useful.

Write over and continue the pattern.

??

Write over and copy the words.

Why? Why?

Write over the words, then put them in the correct order to make a sentence. Copy the sentence below.

did you How ? here get

Write over and copy this question.

Do you like chocolate?

Copy these questions. Can you answer them without saying yes or no?

Would you like sprouts for breakfast?

Do you wear shoes on your head?

Are you the tallest in your family?

Do your question marks take up more space than most letters?

Write over and continue the pattern.

ckıckı

Write over and copy the letters.

ki ke ak ik

Remember to add the dot after joining all the letters.

Write over and copy the words.

king kettle

lake bike

Write over and copy the words.

tick packet

Copy and complete the sentences using the appropriate word from the box.

pocket	rocket	lucky

I flew to the moon in a ____________.

I have got coins in my ____________.

If you are ____________, you will win.

Does ck always come at the end of a word? What are the rules?

Write over and continue the pattern.

tly tly

Write over and copy the letters.

ty ey ay

Write over and copy the words.

party money

eyes staying

Write over and copy the words.

ready myself

Copy the riddle. What colour is it describing? Take extra care with joining to *y*.

My first is in goat but never in coat.

My second is in ray but not in day.

My third is in eye and also in met.

My fourth is in dry but never in wet.

Remember that we join to y but never from it.

Write over and continue the pattern.

bpq bpq

Write over and copy the letters. .

ab ip ag

Remember to add the dot after joining all the letters.

Write over and copy the words.

stable wipe

slipper page

Write over and copy the words.

play jump

Copy the definitions and write the words they are describing (the initial letter is in brackets).

1 The colour of blackcurrant juice (p)

2 Lives at the top of a beanstalk (g)

3 Wibbly wobbly dessert (j)

Remember that you can join to break letters, but not **from** them.

Write over and continue the pattern.

of of

Write over and copy the letters.

of off fo

Write over and copy the words.

often softly

coffee follow

Write over and copy the words.

flat felt

perfect different

Copy the tongue-twister. Can you read it out loud without getting your tongue in a twist?

The five fat frogs

followed the frightful flat fish.

Can you join to and from the letter f correctly?

Write over and continue the pattern.

hij hij

Write over and copy the letters.

ab ac ad ae af ag

Write over and then copy the words in alphabetical order.

action again address

Write over and then copy the words in alphabetical order.

elephant lion deer goat bear

Copy the words, putting each row in alphabetical order.

motorbike car aeroplane

banana breadfruit blueberry

Did you remember to look at the second letter if the first letter was the same?

Write over and continue the pattern.

XPZ XPZ

Write over the capital letters and fill in the gaps. Then copy the complete alphabet below.

A C D F H I J L

N O P Q S T U V W X Y Z

Copy the sentence.

On Friday, Jin and I are going to Earthquest.

Copy the passage, adding all the capital letters.

mr yang asked me to talk about

the african animals at earthquest.

Are all the ascenders the correct height?

Copy the sentences.

I went on my first ever holiday to Wave Town with my friend Livvy. We loved it.

How well do you think you have done in your writing?

Spacing my joins from **v**, **w** and ***f***   

My joins to letter **y**   

My capital letters   

Copy the conversation.

"Where do you live?" asked the lion.
"In a tiny little house," replied the mouse.

How well do you think you have done in your writing?

My joins from **o**   

My **v** joins   

My question mark   

Write over and continue the pattern.

ulul

Write over and copy the letters.

it to

Write over and copy the words.

little fit

told tomorrow

Write over and copy the words.

pattern late

kettle toast

Choose the correct word from the box, then copy the sentence.

metal	fat	token

You need a ________ to go on the ride.

My cat eats so much, it's getting _____.

My new bike is made of shiny ________.

Is your **t** shorter than all the other tall letters?

Write over and continue the pattern.

lolo

Write over and copy the letters.

oo ll rr

Write over and copy the words.

school wooden

spelling narrow

Write over and copy the words.

fluff falling

Copy the poem. Can you guess the colour?

A fluffy chick, a summer sun,

A buttercup hill – roll down for fun.

Lemon jelly – all quiver and quake,

A tall giraffe, a banana shake.

Are your double letters correctly spaced?

Write over and continue the pattern.

ididid

Write over and copy the letters.

ed ng

Write over and copy the words.

red medal

song singing

Write over and copy the words.

played widen

Copy and complete the sentences with the correct tense.

She has row/rowing/rowed the boat.

I am learn/learning/learned French.

I will be sail/sailing/sailed tomorrow.

Do you change direction when you make a diagonal join to a round letter?

Write over and continue the pattern.

szsz

Write over and copy the letters.

sl sh st zo

Write over and copy the words.

asleep washing

stars buzzing

Write over and copy the words.

oxygen staying

Copy the definitions and choose the correct words.

flying	butterfly	xylophone

1 Moving through the air like a bird.

2 A musical instrument with flat bars.

3 A colourful flying insect.

What are the rules about joining b x y z s?

Write over and continue the pattern.

wawa

Write over and copy the letters.

wa oa

Write over and copy the words.

wander swan

toad foal

Write over and copy the words.

woman swoop

Copy the play script. You can choose your own names for the characters.

A: Do you walk home from school?

B: Yes, I walk around the woods.

A: I prefer the road through town.

Remember to keep your pencil on the page when you change direction.

Write over and continue the pattern.

ococ

Write over and copy the letters.

od or ol

Write over and copy the words.

odd order

doctor follow

Write over and copy the words.

doing lower

round rollercoaster

Copy the signs that you might find in a town.

Please do not drop litter on the ground.

No stopping allowed on this road.

Loading and unloading zone for shops only.

Can you join o to and from every letter?

Write over and continue the pattern.

NRK NRK

Write over and copy the letters.

Tu In Ap Ma Ne Ro

Proofread the words below, then copy them out correctly.

tuesday india

marcus april

Write over *i* and *I* in the sentence and then copy the sentence below.

I live in India but I would like to visit Italy.

Proofread the sentences, then copy them out correctly.

jan and i went to spain on holiday.

on fridays, ravi and i play cricket.

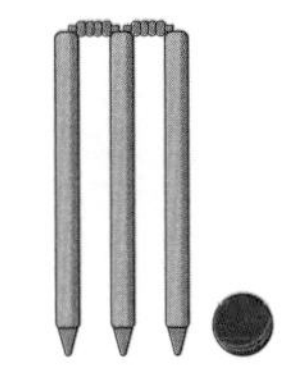

Have you proofread carefully and made changes to all your capital letters?

Write over and continue the pattern.

owow

Write over and copy the letters.

ov va ow

Write over and copy the words.

love moving

vain town

Write over and copy the words.

vent power dove

Copy and complete the sentences using an appropriate word.

flour	love	flowers

I ________ going to the swimming pool.

We need strong white ________.

There are lovely ________ in the park.

Can you think of words where **ou** and **ow** sound the same: for example, cow and loud?

Write over and continue the numbers.

1 2 3 4 5 6 7 8 9 10

Write over and copy the numbers.

one two three

four five six

Write over and copy the numbers.

seven eight nine

Copy and complete the sentences using the appropriate number words.

one two three four five six seven eight nine ten

An octopus has ________ arms, but I have ________.

A dog has ________ legs but an insect has ________.

Can you write these number words from memory?

Copy the sentence.

The little parakeet with the fluffy yellow feathers was too young to fly.

How well do you think you have done in your writing?

My joins to round letters			
The height and spacing of my double letters			
My joins to and from **t** and **o**			

Write the numbers and copy the counting rhyme.

0 1 2 3 4 5 6 7 8 9 10

One, two, three, four,

Five, six, seven and more.

How well do you think you have done in your writing?

My writing of numbers			
My writing of number words